Voyage Of A Lifetime

On The Sea Of Life

By Tom Laiben

Illustrated by Claudia White

A Voyage Of A Lifetime

On The Sea Of Life

All rights reserved. No portion of this book may be reproduced in any form by any means – electronic, mechanical, photocopy, recording or any other ~ except brief quotations, without the written permission of the author.

Author: Tom Laiben

Cover Design: Claudia White

Illustrator: Claudia White

Copyright©2008 by Tom Laiben   ISBN 978-0-557-27307-2

To Jan Laiben, my wife and best friend.

I will never be able to thank God enough

for blessing me with a wife that has always been there for me.

She is my anchor in the storms of life along with our God!.

I would also like to thank Claudia for her great illustrations

that tell their own story and knitted this story together.

Tom Laiben

I saw the carpenter bent over the hull, shaping it into a one-of-a-kind vessel. I asked what he was doing and He replied, "I'm building your boat so you can begin your Voyage of a Lifetime on the Sea of Life."

"But, I'm not a sailor!" I objected. "How do I know what to do or where to go on the Sea of Life?"

In a strong voice He answered, "You will learn by one of two ways: you can learn on your own, by trial and error, or you can let me be your Captain. The choice is yours and yours alone. You have been given the free will to make this decision."

My mind raced with thoughts and questions. *Can I do this by myself?* I will be in charge, with no one to order me around! Or, do I make this voyage with a captain who looks to be only a carpenter, but says He knows the way.

I had two choices and I had my free will. He had given me the vessel and now I had to decide... *my way or His way.*

I checked out my boat and saw that it had two oars and an anchor, and from what I "knew" about boats, that was all I needed. So naturally I thought, How hard can this be? I can figure out something this simple. So I decided to do it *my way*.

Let Me tell you about doing it "my way". I took my boat, my oars, and my anchor and headed out onto the Sea of Life. I had no one telling me what to do, or where to go, and for a while, I thought life was good!

I saw lots of other boats. I saw bigger boats, fancier boats, boats in large groups, boats in small groups, and some boats that were all alone on the Sea of Life.

I saw things that I wanted, or thought I needed. I got or did whatever I thought would make my life better, but my happiness would last for only a short time.

I tried putting different things in, or on my vessel to make it look better or feel more comfortable; but nothing lived up to my expectations. Sometimes the things I got for my boat actually made me feel worse.

One of the greatest challenges of my voyage was being lost. Of course it was easy to get lost because I didn't really know where I was going. When I saw other boats that seemed to know where they were going, I'd ask them for directions.

Some were very helpful and would say, "Sure, we can help you, just follow us!" But, sooner or later, we would all end up lost. I thought they had good direction in their lives, but it was only an illusion.

I ran into terrible storms on the Sea of Life, and I didn't know how to handle them. So, whenever storms came into my path, I would throw my anchor overboard, hunker down and just try to ride it out. I was washed over by giant waves and tossed about so badly that many times I thought my boat would sink to the bottom of the sea! The more I tried to control my life on the sea, the more I knew I needed help. But who could I turn to? None of the other boats were doing any better. I was going in circles and I was going nowhere.

One day, while sitting in a cold drizzle, with fog all around me, I saw a man on the shore. He was just standing there, and he looked like someone I had met before. I began to row towards him. I figured sitting on the shore with a familiar face would be much better than bobbing around in the cold rain all by myself.

As I got closer I realized it was the carpenter, the boat builder, *my boat builder!* In my excitement I began to row faster.

But suddenly I stopped. A fear came over me. I knew then that I'd made the wrong "choice." My thoughts ran wild. What if He was angry because I had chosen to do this my way? What if He said he'd wasted his time building my boat? I doubted that He was happy about the things I had put in it, or where I had been with it, thinking that He probably wanted nothing to do with me...

I was about to turn around and row back into the fog when I looked His way. I saw Him smile and wave to me as if He had just found his child who had been lost for a long, long time. I felt great comfort and warmth, the closer I got to him, the happier He seemed to be!

He began running back and forth on the shore, calling my name, welcoming me home! I felt a great comfort and warmth, and the closer I got to Him, the happier He looked. I thought that once I'd made the decision to go on the Sea of Life without Him, that He would no longer want to be my captain. Now I knew that He had always been waiting for me and was ready to show me the way.

    I finally reached the shore, and I had never been so happy, so filled with joy, so at peace, as when He reached out and gently put his strong carpenter arms around me and said, "Welcome home, I've missed you!" As He pulled me into Him, I thanked Him for waiting for me. And He said, "I never gave up on you. Today I will change you into a new kind of boat and I will give you everything you need to continue your voyage."

As He led me to his shop, I said to Him, "But I thought I only needed an anchor and two oars." Looking back over his shoulder, He replied, "That is all you need if you're content with a rowboat with no direction or destination. But, a large, seaworthy sailboat that can travel to great destinations, needs to be fully equipped. What I am giving you will keep you on course and see you through your storms."

When we reached his shop, He threw open the doors, and I stood in amazement at the endless quantity and variety of all He had stored there!

He began handing me my new supplies. He gave me two large poles, planks of wood, coil after coil of thick heavy rope, a huge piece of strong canvas, and a lifejacket.

Lastly, He placed a compass in my hands. It was gold, inlaid with pearl, and was the most beautiful thing that I had ever seen. Holding the compass brought the same joy to me as the smile on his face and the comfort of his arms had done earlier.

After everything was loaded on my deck, I asked Him, "I know you're a carpenter and soon to be my captain, but just who are you?"

That's when a cloud appeared, and a voice came from the cloud: "This is My Son, whom I love. Listen to Him!" Then the carpenter said, "Remember, I'm the one who made you. I am your Captain. I am your Savior."

After taking stock of all the supplies He had given me, I asked Him, "Is this everything I need for this voyage on the Sea of Life?" His reply was, "This is all you need to get started."

"But," I questioned, "what if I *want* something else?" "I will always see that your needs are met," He assured me. "Now let's rig this boat and get you on your way!"

He began giving me instructions on the placement of the longer of the two poles. "Cut a hole in your deck and place it down into your keel and then attach the shorter pole like this. These two wooden poles are your mast and it needs to be the strongest part of your sailboat. It is what the sail and the ropes are attached to. Now that you have come back to Me, you should remain at the foot of the mast for the rest of your life!"

I told Him that it looked like a cross, and He said, "Yes, it is a cross and it's where I gave my life so that you could become a new vessel with a promise!"

"What promise?" I asked. He said that when we finished rigging my boat, the promise would be revealed.

"Okay, what's next?" I asked. "Now, attach the rope to the mast. This rope holds the mast to the vessel and ties the sail to the mast," He answered. When I asked what the rope was made of and what made it so strong, He told me, "The rope is made from every word given from the Father and used to write the Holy Scriptures.

The Old and New Testaments are intertwined, and every word is important. Never let one part of the rope become more important or stronger than the others because that's when it can begin to unravel.

"Now, attach the sail to the mast using the rope," He directed.

"What's the sail made of and what does it do?" I asked. "It is the Sail of Faith, and the more you trust and believe, the bigger and stronger your sail will become," He explained.

As He handed me the lifejacket, I wondered if He was growing weary of all my questions. He must have guessed my thoughts, because without my asking, He told me,

"Everybody needs a lifejacket. It keeps you afloat and safe through life's storms. It is your salvation and guarantees eternal life. Never remove it!"

My eyes fell on the compass. I picked it up and again marveled at its beauty. He gently took it from me. He held it up and light reflected from it. "This is the compass of the Holy Spirit, who will direct and guide you for the duration of your voyage. It is equipped with an alarm that will sound off anytime you are getting off course. Listen closely. It's usually easy to hear, but at times, it will be no more than a whisper."

He then led me to the back of the boat and showed me the rudder. "What will I use this for?" His answer surprised me. "Even though I am your captain you still have your free will. The rudder directs the sailboat and steers it in the direction you want to go. You need to stay focused on the compass and follow its lead. Listen for the alarm to alert you that you are straying from the course. You can have the biggest boat and the largest sail, but still be headed in the wrong direction. Keep your eyes and ears on the compass at all times because your hand will always be on your rudder of free will."

Finally, He attached a large new anchor. I pointed out that I already had an anchor. He turned from his task and began to explain, "The size of the anchor must match the size of the boat. This anchor will hold you fast and secure in any situation.

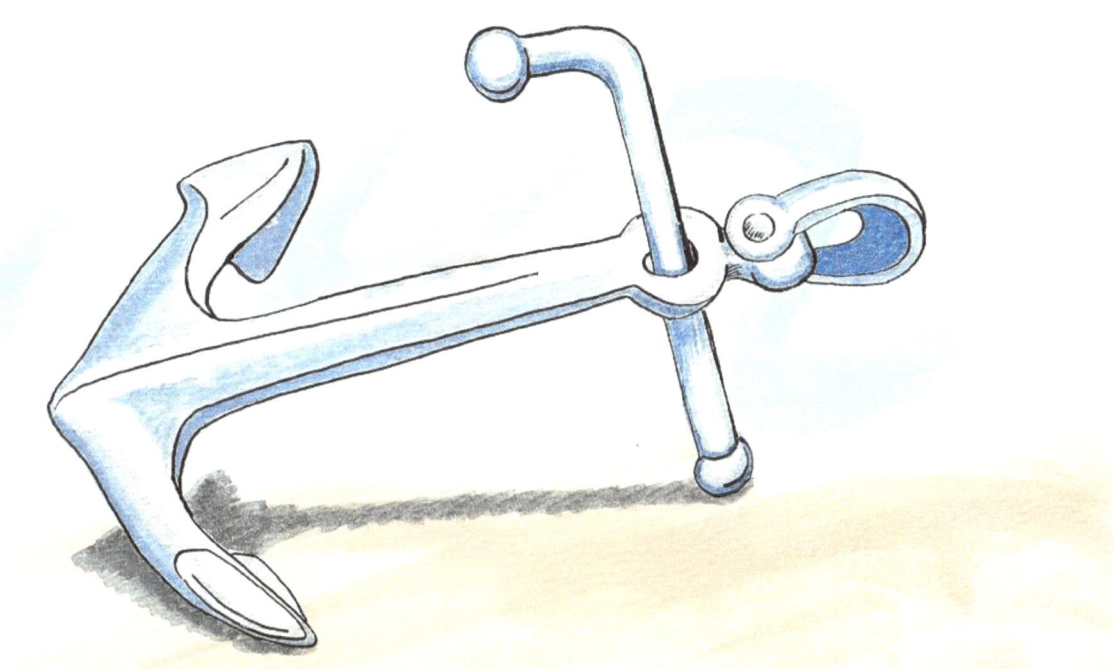

It's made of something that is much, much stronger than anything ever made by man. I give you an anchor of love, joy, peace, patience, kindness, goodness, faithfulness, and self-control. None of life's storms are stronger than your anchor. Rest assured that it will hold!"

He stood back, took a long look and then told me that my boat was fully equipped and that I was ready to continue my voyage. I looked over the side into the calm waters and saw my reflection. I saw a perfectly crafted, beautifully unique sailboat.

I turned to look at Him and there was a big smile on his face. "You have everything you need. It's time to go." I, of course, had one more question, "I don't know how to move without my oars. What do I do?"

"Simple." He replied,..

"God, My Father, will send His wind to fill your Sail of Faith. Let Him keep your sails full and open, and you will journey far and experience incredible things. Maintain the strength of the ropes, keep your eyes and ears on the compass, and your hand on the rudder. When you see someone whose oars are missing or whose anchor is stuck or someone who's lost, toss them a rope and bring them to Me. I will be waiting for them. Just like I was waiting for you. I have made you a unique vessel, equipped with your own gifts and passions. Now begin your great Voyage on the Sea of Life."

...I think I'm ready, but there is one last thing. You said that you would reveal ..*'The Promise'* to me."

    Our Lord Jesus then turned to me and said, "My promise to you is one of salvation. I promise that you can come to Me, regardless of your circumstances. I care nothing for your past – only your future. If you would like to receive Me as your savior, say this simple prayer: "I am a sinner, but I believe that God sent His Son, Jesus Christ, to die for my sins – past, present and future. I believe Jesus rose from the grave and sits at the right hand of The Father. I believe I will one day be with Him in Heaven. Amen."

Congratulations! You have just made the decision to follow Christ.

Tom and Claudia urge you to ask friends and family to help you find a local church

to fellowship and grow in your spiritual walk as you continue your new life in Jesus Christ.

Many Blessings to you, and Welcome to the Family!

~for your records~

Name _____

Date of Decision _____

About The Author

Gerald (Tom) Laiben is the father of Daniel and Kristie Sessions. He lives in Florida, along with his wife Jan. Tom is a house painter and server at his church as Lay Pastor.

About The Illustrator

Claudia White is a wife and mother of five children. She resides in Northwest Florida. She began drawing as a child and continued her art through out her lifetime working in advertising, commercial art, and illustrations. Her talents are widely used serving in her church for children & youth ministry, as well as VBS and Church Display and set designs.

www.ingramcontent.com/pod-product-compliance
Lightning Source LLC
Chambersburg PA
CBHW041552220426
43666CB00002B/47